HOCKEY MOMS AREN'T CRAZY!

by
Jody M. Anderson,
artwork by Phil Juliano

LAKE7 CREATIVE llc

Minneapolis, Minnesota

The jokes in this book came from my own experiences raising three hockey players. I also borrowed ideas from many of my Hockey Mom friends, who so willingly shared them with me. I rounded out the book by putting a new spin on some of those old and retold jokes we've heard a hundred times before. I would like to thank my family, friends, players, coaches, trainers, and all who shared Hockey Mom memories that made this book possible. I would also like to thank Lake 7 Creative for believing in my project. Without you, none of this would've happened!

The illustrations in this book were created by Phil Juliano, based on original artwork from the imagination of Scott Rolfs. Any resemblance to real persons, living or dead, is purely coincidental.

Edited and designed by Ryan Jacobson
Cover design by Y. Shane Nitzsche
Footer illustration by twggy/Shutterstock.com

10 9 8 7 6 5 4 3 2 1

First edition 2013 | Second edition 2022
Copyright 2013, 2022 by Jody M. Anderson
Published by Lake 7 Creative, LLC
Minneapolis, MN 55412
www.lake7creative.com

ISBN: 978-1-940647-63-0
eISBN: 978-1-940647-64-7

This book is dedicated to all
Hockey Moms, everywhere!

—Jody M. Anderson

Follow Jody M. Anderson on Social Media:

FaceBook: HockeyMomsArentCrazy

Instagram: Hockey_Moms_Arent_Crazy

TikTok: @jody_hockeymom

Twitter: @HockeyMom_Jody

FOREWORD

My mom was the perfect Hockey Mom, and that's why she's a great candidate to write this book. I played hockey for 10 years, and my mom barely ever missed a game. I think she might have been more dedicated than I was! My mom was my biggest supporter, bringing me to morning practices at 5:30 a.m., always pushing me to do my best, and never letting me give up.

I had a really tough senior year in high school, and I didn't know if I wanted to keep playing. But my mom told me to keep going. I don't know what I would've done without my mom during hockey. She did everything possible to keep me positive.

I want to thank her for never giving up on me and never letting me give up on hockey. Love ya, Mom!

—Katie Anderson,
Hockey Daughter

INTRODUCTION BY JODY ANDERSON

When my son Jeremy was in the second grade, he came home with a paper for hockey sign-up at the local school. He was so excited; how could I say no? Little did I know it would lead to a life of volunteering to bring treats, becoming the hockey manager, writing the bylaws and articles of incorporation for the girls' high school team . . . We also gained a lifelong obsession with hockey!

As I reflect back on my life as a Hockey Mom, I remember all the family time we spent together and all the friends we made. At the end of every season, we always had a parents-versus-kids game. It was a blast. Those kids played harder against us than they did all year! (It's still always a debate about who won those games.)

Of course, if there's one thing about Hockey Moms, it's that we have stories. I've shared so many tales about hockey, the kids, the coaches, and the tournaments that one day someone said, "You need to write a book!"

After thinking about it for a while, I decided it was a great idea. But not just for me. I wanted to make a tribute to all Hockey Moms out there.

I started sharing book ideas with other moms, which led to interviews not only with Hockey Moms but also with the players themselves. They seemed to relish the opportunity to say how important their Hockey Moms were—and still are—to them. Next, I took my idea to social media, and I got a lot of positive responses.

I was on Twitter one night, and a tweet by Mike Eruzione (perhaps most famously known as the captain of the 1980 United States Winter Olympics Hockey Team) alerted me that he happened to be online too. So I thought, "What the heck? I'll zap him a tweet and see if I can get a story or two about his mom." I told him about the book and that I'd love to include a story about his mom. He got right back to me and said yes; I was shocked!

Two days later, Mike Eruzione called me, and I almost had a heart attack. He wanted to do the interview right then and there, but I told him I was in no way prepared for him! He was very understanding, and we set up an appointment for a later time. I then proceeded to drive to an eye appointment, but the doctor couldn't do the appointment because my blood pressure was so high. I explained, "You have no idea who I just talked to!"

As that story demonstrates, I'm still as passionate as ever about hockey. We attend as many games as possible; it's a family thing with us. I'm not a Hockey Mom anymore, though. I've graduated to Hockey Grandma. Yay! With this book, I hope to bring back pleasant memories for all Hockey Moms and perhaps even provide a laugh or two. Enjoy the book!

—Jody M. Anderson,
Hockey Mom

INTRODUCTION BY MICHAEL RUSSO

I don't play hockey.

Can barely skate.

My mom didn't have to wake up at ungodly hours during the winter months and trek me to the rinks all over the state.

She didn't have to toss my sweaty clothes in the washer and hang my gear in the garage so it didn't smell up the house. She didn't have to hold her breath every time I got checked and never got the elation of cheering when her son scored a big goal, made a nice pass, or a pulled off a clutch save.

But make no mistake, I have a Hockey Mom too.

"What's going on with Kaprizov?"

"What's the latest with Fiala?"

"How's Parise doing with the Islanders?"

"When's the last time you talked to Backstrom?"

"Do you believe Gaudreau signed with Columbus?"

I'm a hockey writer, and my mom's been my biggest fan, well, forever.

I started as a sportswriter at age 15, began covering the NHL and the Florida Panthers in 1995—and here we are in 2022, and I'm still covering the league and the Minnesota Wild.

Nobody, and I mean nobody, knows more about the Wild than my mom, Barbara. She reads every word I write, listens to—and believes!—every word I say on radio, TV, and podcasts.

It's her way of having a relationship with me.

It's always been this way.

I remember when I was in my 20s, I'd get my mom and stepdad, Lenny, tickets to a Panthers game. All game long, while Lenny didn't take his eyes off the ice, my mom didn't take her eyes off the press box.

Watching, staring at me while I worked.

I could see her smile from 200 yards away. It was kinda distracting, in all honesty.

But it warmed my heart.

In 2014, when Lenny—my other "biggest fan," somebody who used to drive me to high school football games when I was too young to drive at night and then sit in the newsroom and wait for me as I wrote, somebody who cut out every article I penned and pasted them in scrapbooks—died, my heartbroken mother really became the biggest Wild fan ever. It was her way to cope, gave her something to do, a way to grieve and distract herself from the sorrow at night.

I'm not kidding, I don't think she has missed a single Wild game since 2014.

And inevitably, after she fills my phone with a load of texts during the game and after she reads my article the next morning, she'll call me up and want to discuss every detail of the game, my article, and what the fans are saying in the comments section.

Again, it's her way of supporting me and talking to me about something she knows I'm passionate about.

She's so proud of herself when she gives me a take and I agree. She's prolific on Twitter, too, as I often notice that she likes every single tweet of every single fan that says anything nice about me.

She doesn't know I can see this, but I can and it always makes me giggle.

There's just something comforting about always knowing, on the toughest days of this job, there's at least one fan whom I can do no wrong with.

That's what a Hockey Mom does: supports her son or daughter, whatever their dreams, whether it's strapping up the skates and playing the great sport of hockey . . . or writing about it.

There's something special about the Hockey Mom, which is why I so love this book.

Enjoy this great collection of funny and informative stories about a tight-knit, special community of Hockey Moms.

—Michael Russo,
Sports Journalist,
The Athletic

A GOALIE'S JOB

When my son Rio started playing hockey, he was three years old and in the iprogram. He was by far the youngest one. Before the end-of-year tournament, all the kids, the coach, and parents were in the locker room. The coach was giving the kids their little pump-up speech before their first game ever.

He held up the puck and asked, "What is this?"

They all screamed, "Puck!"

The coach said, while holding up the puck, "The main goal of the game is to get the puck in the net."

We quickly realized that my son, being three years old, didn't understand that the goalie was supposed to keep the puck *out* of the net. Granted, they never really practiced playing goalie. However, the other kids were old enough to understand.

Coach said, "Everyone is taking a turn at goalie."

Rio's turn was first. He skated away from the net and joined the game. We were all saying to each other, "What is he doing?" We were all pointing and screaming, "Go back to the net!"

Well, with his little three-year-old eyes, he thought everyone was waving. So what did he do? Wave back to everyone—and he helped the other team score! Of course, the stands were roaring with laughter.

After the game, we asked him, "Why did you join the game and leave the net?"

Rio said in his little lispy voice, "Coach said the main goal of the game is to get the puck in the net."

We went home and practiced that night to make sure he understood his job as a goalie. The following day, for the next game, he did much better as goalie and did what a goalie is supposed to do.

—Melanie,
Hockey Mom

FAMILY LOVE

Child: Mom, would you still love me if I didn't play hockey?

. . . Mom, did you hear me?

Mom: Yes, of course, dear.

Child: You'd still love me?

Mom: No, I meant I heard you.

Child: Well, would you?

Mom: Don't rush me. I'm thinking.

★ ★ ★

Soccer Mom: When my kids are naughty, I give them a timeout.

Hockey Mom: When my kids are naughty, I put them in the penalty box!

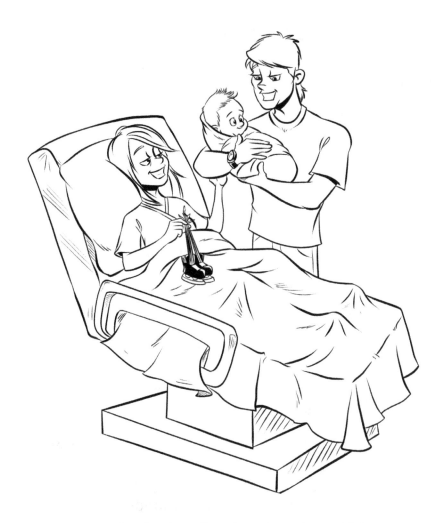

Dad: Our daughter is so beautiful.

Hockey Mom: Oh, she's a blessing. She's a joy.
Now put these on her.

OH, THOSE KIDS!

Child: Are the lakes frozen yet? Are they? Are they?

Mom: Sweetie, it's August.

★ ★ ★

Dad: Son, why do you have black marker all over your face?

Son: Playoff beard!

★ ★ ★

Mom: I can't believe you burned down the garage!

Son: It was an accident, Mom. I didn't mean to do it.

Mom: I don't care! You're grounded for a month . . . except to play hockey.

Mom: Yep, now you're a hockey player.

SCHOOL DAYS

Suzie: My report today is about Judy Johnson.

Teacher: Suzie, your report is supposed to be about a president.

Suzie: It is. She's president of our Parent Hockey Association.

★ ★ ★

Teacher: Coach, don't tell me you're already scouting my students. They're only in first grade!

Coach: Well, some of them have potential, but they need to show more focus.

★ ★ ★

You might be a Hockey Mom if . . . your son always wears a hockey belt, even with a tuxedo.

Mom: You're getting your homework done, right? What are you studying?

Daughter: Um . . . history.

Pockets

Last year, our four-year-old, Tara, started a program that teaches her how to play hockey. I was helping her get ready while my husband, Zac, was loading the dishwasher. As I helped her pull her new pants over her long johns, she realized that the pants had pockets.

She excitedly yelled, "Daddy, now I have a pocket for my lip gloss!"

Zac quickly answered, "No! There's no lip gloss in hockey!"

I guess a girl needs lip gloss, even when she's on the ice.

—Kylah Eckes,
Hockey Mom

Tara: Daddy, now I have a pocket for my lip gloss!

Daddy: No! There's no lip gloss in hockey!

THE COED TEAM

We lived in Seattle, where my daughter Nadya played in a girls' league in the Canadian Pacific League. We moved to Massachusetts before Nadya entered eighth grade. Winter sports club came around, and she wanted to play for her coed middle school team to meet new kids. Sure thing! We signed her up.

It was a blustery, dark Friday night and the doorbell rang. We were new to town and didn't know anyone. So I reluctantly opened the door, and there was a man standing there.

"Hello, I'm looking for Nadya's parents."

I answered, "I'm her mom. How can I help you?"

He responded, "I'm the middle school hockey manager, and I know you're new to town. I saw that your daughter signed up for coed hockey."

My guard came down, and I invited him inside.

He said, "I also wanted to let you know that the middle school league is coed, and they do permit checking."

My answer was, "Okay, so is there a problem?"

"No, but wanted you to be aware of the checking policy."

I said. "Let me introduce you to my daughter." Then I called, "Nadya, can you please come here for an minute?"

She came into the entry, and the coach's jaw dropped.

He said, "Yeah, you 'll be fine," while looking at my 6-foot-tall 13-year-old.

—Kathleen Payeur,
Hockey Mom

SHOOTING GOALIE

During a game, a child on the opposing team was skating down to try and score a goal. Our little goalie was too busy to see this guy because he was using his hockey stick as a pretend gun to shoot imaginary ducks!

Yes, the guy scored and won the game for his team.

—Anonymous,
Hockey Mom

Coach: Your kid knows that's just an expression, right?

Tweet, Tweet

Our Twitter group tweeted at a Hockey Mom whom we wanted to meet: "Can we get together between periods to introduce ourselves?"

"Sure," she answered.

"How will we know you?" we asked.

She answered, "Look for the cute, short, masked lady who once gave birth to the huge goalie!"

We knew at that point we'd have fun getting to know her! We saw her several more times during the season. She had two goalies at the state tournament! How could she possibly stay sane? But somehow she did!

—Twitter-Famous
Hockey Mom Fans

Dad: Are you ready to go?

Mom: I don't know. Do you think the earrings are too much?

Dad: Uh, yeah, it's the earrings.

Hockey Kids

Mom #1: Are you going to have more children?

Mom #2: Yes, but we're going to plan it just right. We want our next child to have a good hockey birthday.

Mom #1: We want more kids so we can start 'em younger!

✦ ✦ ✦

Husband: Why do you always laugh when someone tells you that their kids play soccer?

✦ ✦ ✦

You might be a Hockey Mom if . . . you've ever said to your child, "No, I don't want to smell your gloves."

Mom: You play hockey?

Boy: Yes, ma'am.

Mom: Keep her out as late as you want.

Mom's Game

Back in the mid-1970s, I was playing goalie for the local Junior A team. My mother was from Croatia and lived through World War II. She carried a lot of fear with her and was against me playing any sport—let alone goaltending in ice hockey. She would carry on while I packed my equipment bag and would say rosaries. But when I got home, she would want details of the game.

She was sick. She had kidney issues, which eventually required a transplant. After that, she became more active and expressed an interest in going to one of my games. So, one day, out of the clear blue, she announced that she was coming to my game, along with my dad.

The rink was packed that afternoon. I remember taking the ice, but I couldn't find mom in the stands. I remember a scuffle breaking out in front of me while I was trying to freeze a loose puck. A kid slashed my glove, and I completely lost it. It was a highlight fight, and I clobbered the guy. I got a game misconduct.

As I was making my way off the ice, I saw a huge fight breaking out in the stands. I learned later that it was my mother who started it. It turned out that the woman sitting next to her was the mother of the kid I clobbered.

Dad said he'd never seen anything like it. He said she exchanged words with the woman, in broken English, and before he could step in, my mom had her in a headlock and was pulling her hair and punching her. Mom's first ice hockey game got her banned from the rink! She never had alcohol in her life, but that night she was drinking beer and dropping F-bombs. I guess hockey has a way of bringing out your primal self.

I remember we watched the Philadelphia Flyers play the Soviet Red Army team. I couldn't understand why my mom was cheering for the Russians until later in life. The Russians drove the Germans out of the town she lived in as a small girl.

—Michael Anthony,
Inventor of the OneZee Goalie Helmet

ON THE RUN

When you have four kids, being a Hockey Mom isn't easy. For example, it was challenging to really focus on the ice. While watching my Mite 3 son on the rink, I took my eyes off the one-and-a-half-year-old, Morrey. I didn't realize that, in the two seconds I looked away, my speedy little toddler had made a run for it.

I frantically started looking around, and some little puck chasers told me that he ran into the women's bathroom. I found him in a stall with his head in the toilet. I tried to pull him out, but his head actually got stuck in the seat! I had to maneuver it through the opening.

Toilet water dripped from his wet hair down my arms. But I did not go home to immediately bathe him. Instead, like any true Hockey Mom would do, I ran back to the rink with my toilet-soaked toddler to cheer on my Mite!

—Jenny,
Hockey Mom

Boy: The locker room smells like your mom's minivan!

Pet Names

Boards	Bobby
Boxer	Brawler
Breakaway	Checkers
Crease	Dangle
Deke	Easton
Goalie	Goldie
Goon	Gordie
Gretzky	Hat Trick (or Trixie)
Hockey	Icy
Mario	Mullet
Netter	Puck
Skater	Slapshot
Stanley	Winger
Yzerman	Zamboni

You might be a Hockey Mom if . . . you even have to tell your pet to "get out of the way" when there's a hockey game on TV.

HOCKEY BAG

With the kids' school and hockey schedules, life could be a bit crazy as we rushed from one thing to the next.

There was one evening when I received a call from my son Dougie's team manager. He told me that I needed to come to the arena right away. Apparently, when Dougie opened his bag in the locker room, a surprise popped its head out. It was GiGi, our pet ferret!

The team thought it was the best thing to have that cute, furry animal in the locker room. But, unfortunately, GiGi was quite a distraction and needed to go home.

—Joni Zine,
Hockey Mom

When Dougie opened his bag in the locker
room, a surprise popped its head out.

Lesson Learned

It was the start of the game, and my son was ready to go. The puck was dropped, and my son and a boy from the other team ran into each other. They both fell, and I laughed.

Then I saw my son get up, and I knew it wasn't going to be good. He was not happy. He swung his stick and hit the kid. Needless to say, he was benched for the remainder of the game.

Afterwards, I walked down to the locker room, and my son was waiting for me. I just looked at him and didn't say a word.

I gave him a hug and told him that I loved him, but the car ride home was a long lesson on what he cannot do in hockey.

—Crystal Ziebarth,
Hockey Mom

PLAYING HURT

I was watching my son play hockey at the pee-wee level. On his first shift, he was slammed into the corner boards. He finished his shift and went back to the bench, shaking his hand. He took off his glove and sprayed water on his hand. He played the entire game, but every once in a while, he'd shake his hand in pain.

"Something's wrong with Jeremy's hand," I said to my husband.

At the end of the game, Jeremy came up the steps, showed me his thumb, and said, "I think I broke my thumb."

I took a look, and his thumb was bent the wrong way! I asked him why he didn't tell his coach.

His response was, "If I did, he wouldn't have let me play."

—Jody M. Anderson,
Hockey Mom

Free Time

Friend: We should get together some time. Do you have plans this weekend?

Mom: Practice.

Friend: How about next weekend?

Mom: Practice.

Friend: And the weekend after that?

Mom: Practice . . .

★ ★ ★

Mom #1: Are you going to the game this weekend?

Mom #2: I'm not sure. I'll have to see if this is one of the rinks my husband is barred from.

Dad: I know we spend a lot of time with the other parents, but this is ridiculous!

"HOCKEY MOM"

I grew up in Detroit in the 1940s and '50s. Back in those days, there was no such thing as a Hockey Mom.

My mom wasn't able to be very involved in the sports side of my life. I don't think she saw me play until I was 16. But I'll always know that, with my mom's support, I was able to get out and play sports.

—Carl Wetzel,
Hockey Pro
1958–1973

Mom: You can do it! Go! Go! Go!

Stranger: Ma'am, this is a piano recital.

FIGHTING MAD

I have been in the hockey scene for 11 years, and nothing has come close to how embarrassed I was after one of my son's 16U games against an out-of-state team.

In the last minute of the game, there was a lot of fighting on the ice, but it stopped when the buzzer went off and the game was over. As I was walking toward the players who were coming off the ice, my son (one of the smaller players on the team) was behind the other team. His teammates were already on their way to the locker room, and my son got pushed hard by a kid from the other team. Four of their other players were about to get in on this fight. (I'm sure my son mumbled something stupid, which caused him to get shoved.)

I reached behind my son and held him back as I screamed as loud as I could, "That's my son! Stop it!"

My husband heard my scream from across the rink and ran over to us. He held the other kids back, and luckily a dad from the other team told those boys to get in their locker room.

I was very shaken up. But in the parking lot, I met a family that was serving mimosas out of their trunk. They let me have one.

Since then, I have learned to walk away if I see any kind of fighting because I have no clue how I will react—especially if it's my son.

—Jen Izenstark,
Hockey Mom

REACT FIRST

My mom is a full-blooded Yugoslavian, so she's kind of ornery. Most of my memories of her are high-tempered. My mom was one who always reacted and then thought about it afterward. But she was dedicated, committed, giving, and caring. And she always gave you a good meal.

She loved and supported her kids, and she played an important role. She was the head of the household in some ways. Growing up, it was the most important dynamic of the family. She was always there for us. My mom was one of the best—very supportive.

—Mike Peluso,
Hockey Pro
1989–1998

Mom: Okay, I'll pay for this stuff, but I get half of your first pro contract. Do we have a deal?

TECHNOLOGY

Dad: Do you know what time the game starts?

Mom: No, but I can find out. I have the coach on speed dial.

✦ ✦ ✦

A boss was sitting in his office at work. Every so often, he thought he heard the sound of a hockey goal score. After hearing it for the third time, he stormed out of his office.

"You people should be working, but I can hear someone watching hockey! I want to know who it is," he demanded.

A Hockey Mom in the corner raised her hand. "No one's watching hockey, sir. That's just my cell phone's ring tone."

✦ ✦ ✦

Mom: Wow, I had a really busy day at work. I received more than 200 emails!

Dad: How many of them weren't about hockey?

Cashier: Evenin' ma'am. What'll it be?

Mom: I'll have the usual.

Hockey Psychic

A man at a youth hockey game declared to all the Hockey Moms, "I'm a psychic, and I'll bet any of you a dollar that I can guess your computer password."

Several of the Hockey Moms jumped out of their seats and quickly lined up to take that bet.

The first mom in line waved her dollar bill and said, "Take a guess."

"I'll be happy to," replied the psychic. "But first you must tell me your child's name."

The woman smiled proudly and said, "Tommy Matson."

The man picked up a program and scanned it for a moment.

"There he is," said the psychic. "He's number 47, yes?"

The Hockey Mom hesitated, then nodded.

"Your password is hockey47," declared the psychic.

The woman handed him the dollar. Everyone behind her jumped out of line and sat down.

✦ ✦ ✦

Dad: You know he's the coach, right?

Mom: Yes.

Dad: That he's a volunteer?

Mom: Yes.

Dad: That he donates hundreds of hours of his personal time?

Mom: Yes.

Dad: It's still okay to complain about him?

Mom: Yes.

IT'S HOW MUCH?

Child: Mom, I need a new hockey stick.

Mom: At those prices, you better have a good reason for needing one.

Child: Mine doesn't have any more goals in it.

Mom: I'll grab my purse.

✡ ✡ ✡

Banker: Well, ma'am, we can qualify you for a loan of $10,000. Will that be enough?

Mom: No, unfortunately, it won't. I have to pay this year's hockey expenses.

✡ ✡ ✡

Mom: It's time to pay the big bill again.

Dad: Oh, is the mortgage due?

Mom: No, ice fees.

Mom: And I call this one "$600 down the drain."

DREAM HOME

Jim and Cheri were huge hockey fans. In fact, when they decided to buy a house, they only wanted one that a hockey family had lived in. The realtor took them to view the first house.

Without even going inside, Cheri said, "Not this one."

The realtor brought them to the second house.

Before they entered, Cheri said, "Not this one either."

The realtor was sure they'd love the third house, but without even getting out of her minivan, Cheri said, "No way. A hockey family didn't live here either."

The realtor shrugged. "I don't understand, ma'am. Are you psychic?"

Cheri laughed. "Why on earth would you think that?"

"How else could you know that none of these are hockey homes?" asked the realtor.

"Did you see the garages?" Cheri answered. "There's not a single puck dent on 'em!"

✦ ✦ ✦

Mom: How much is the stick you want?

Child: About $180.

Mom: Okay, let's get it.

Child: Should we pick up a birthday card for Dad?

Mom: Are you joking? I'm not spending $5 for that!

EARLY BIRD

My mom is not a morning person, so 6:30 a.m. practices were not her favorite. However, being the best Hockey Mom ever, she always got me there and then took me to Country Kitchen for breakfast prior to school.

Our traditional early-bird breakfast made me late for school, which was a bonus!

I love you, Mom!

—Jeff Nielsen,
Hockey Pro
1994–2001

Mom: Are you ready for breakfast, dear?

Dad: It's 4:00 in the morning!

Mom: I'm a Hockey Mom. This is when
I always eat.

PRACTICE

Child: Mom, the coach doesn't want you attending practice anymore.

Mom: Why not?

Child: There have been complaints.

Mom: About me? Why?

Child: Because you yell, "Watch this!" to the other parents every time I get the puck.

✦ ✦ ✦

You might be a Hockey Mom if . . . any time you're away on business, your child must leave a detailed list of instructions for his dad. Otherwise, your husband won't get him to practice on time!

Mom #1: Can . . . you believe . . . it's only . . . 5 a.m.?

Mom #2: There's . . . no place . . . I'd rather . . . be.

Ice Time

Mom #1: How come your husband always lets you choose where to sit?

Mom #2: So he can sit on the opposite side of the arena.

★ ★ ★

Mom #1: What are you doing?

Mom #2: Keeping stats, of course.

Mom #1: But . . . this is practice.

★ ★ ★

You might be a Hockey Mom if . . . you can name every kid on the ice, but you have no idea who any of your child's classmates are.

Coach: I hate to tell you this, but the odds of a child making it to the pros are something like 1 in 100,000.

Mom: Oh, I know. I feel kinda bad for the other 99,999 kids.

NOT MY KID?

I can picture my father yelling over the front seat of the car, but my mom was a calming influence. She'd say things like, "You weren't bad. Everything was good." She evened out my dad.

I also remember Parents' Night in Duluth, Minnesota. My mom got out of sequence, and she started walking out in front of the crowd with the wrong player. That was embarrassing for her; she had to hurry back and find me!

I thank my mom for raising me with the morals and values that she instilled in me, which shaped me as a hockey player. If I was afraid to tell my mom about it, I knew I shouldn't be doing it. It helped me to make good decisions and to be a leader on the team for the guys.

—Sean Toomey,
Hockey Pro
1986–1989

CHOSEN SONS

Living in Minnesota with three sons and a husband—who was still playing as well as coaching hockey—I didn't have a choice: I was a Hockey Mom! Our middle son was drafted for his first travel team, for which my husband was the coach. At the first practice, all the moms sat together. It quickly became a bragging competition.

"My son was chosen, as he was the leading scorer for his team."

"My son was chosen because he didn't allow any goals."

After a while, I finally spoke up. "I know exactly why my son made the team. I slept with the coach."

There was about 15 seconds of dead silence. Then one mom finally asked, "Are you the coach's wife?"

I responded with a smile.

—Barbara Goldberg,
Hockey Mom

GOOD CALL

I was reffing a game when a team from a big school was beating a much smaller school, 9–1, after two periods. It was a pretty crummy game, actually. Late in the period, the big-school coach asked me if I saw a tripping call.

I said, "What penalty?" I couldn't believe he was worried about a tripping call in a 9–1 game.

He said, "The one down in the corner."

"Was it in front of me or my partner?" I asked.

"In front of your partner," he replied.

I said, "How do you expect me to see that? I'm watching the moms!"

To that, he only answered, "Touché."

—Dave Druk
10-Year District 10
Hockey Official

Mom: What are you supposed to be?

Child: A hockey ref.

Mom: Wow, that is scary.

CHAMPION!

My son, Derek Plante, was able to experience the ultimate goal of every young hockey player: that of becoming a professional.

In 1999, Derek was traded to Dallas just before the playoffs. They kept winning and pretty soon it was the final round. We drove down to Dallas for the sixth game of the championship series.

The final, winner-take-all game was in Buffalo, which we could not fly to. We drove up to Des Moines, Iowa, rented a motel room, and watched from there. Dallas won!

The trophy came to our hometown. There was a picture and autograph session at the old high school rink. Then we had a private party for family and friends, and we drank champagne from the cup. I was a very proud mom!

—Anne Gullion,
Hockey Mom

NEW TACKS

I told my mother that I needed a new pair of Tacks when I was in my last year of high school. She said to quit hockey and concentrate on becoming a dentist. So I had to go to my dad to get them.

—Lou Nanne,
Hall-of-Fame
Hockey Legend

Permission

Dear Mr. Rudy,

Please excuse Jeremy's absence from school yesterday. That new hockey movie was released in theaters, and he couldn't wait to see it.

Sincerely,

Jeremy's Mom

Dad: I don't understand. Why do you get so lonely during the off-season?

Mom: I miss the other parents!

You might be a Hockey Mom if . . . your dust rags are all made from old hockey socks.

Mom: Honey, I didn't think your tux was right for prom. I got you this one instead.

HOCKEY FAMILY

My husband and I named our son Coyle. It comes from a vehicle part (coil) because my husband is a mechanic and from the former Minnesota Wild star Charlie Coyle (our favorite player).

When our Coyle started walking, we put him in skates and covered our hardwood floors with mats. When our town iced the rinks, we took him out on his skates. We also attended Minnesota Wild games and watched the team on TV. I remember taking Coyle to a free outdoor practice. I held him against the glass when goalie Darcy Kemper skated over to us. He tossed a signed puck over the glass. It's a memory I'll never forget.

When Coyle turned two, we tried potty training him. He wasn't ready, but Coyle wanted to skate like the players.

Around the time Coyle turned three, I explained to him that if he wanted to play hockey, he had to be potty trained. It worked! So we signed Coyle up for hockey, and he was the youngest on the team. He was playing with kids who were eight years old.

In 2019, we won tickets to a Wild game. Coyle and I went early to fist bump the players coming out of the tunnel. We watched Charlie Coyle play his final game with the Wild. The next day, he was traded to the Boston Bruins. So we got Coyle Bruins jerseys. When our son skates, he supports both the Wild and the Bruins with his jerseys.

Coyle still works his butt off and enjoys the company of his teammates. It has been rewarding, watching him do what he enjoys. We added another sibling (a brother) for Coyle to play with and teach hockey. We also found out that we're expecting our third child (a girl) around Thanksgiving. We're thrilled to expand our hockey family.

Being a Hockey Mom is a lot of work, keeps us busy, is fun, and makes me proud. I wouldn't change this experience for the world. I encourage other families to sign their kids up for the sport.

— Merissa Menge,
Hockey Mom

CAR TROUBLES

Mom #1: My husband still drives his car from 1968. It has nearly 400,000 miles on it!

Mom #2: That's nothin'. I have a 2018 SUV . . . and I'm a Hockey Mom!

✦ ✦ ✦

Dad: You know, you're not very good at giving people directions.

Mom: Why? Because I'm a woman?

Mom: No, because your directions are always based on the closest hockey arena.

✦ ✦ ✦

Mom #1: How old are your children?

Mom #2: I have a '90 and a '93. And you?

Mom #1: A '95 and a '97.

Mom: I don't know, dear. Do you think we'll ever find the right vehicle?

Dad: What's wrong with this one?

Mom: It's not big enough!

FAMILY TIME

Dad: There's a hockey tournament in Wisconsin Dells. You know what that means, right?

Mom: Family vacation!

★ ★ ★

Girl: I brought my school picture for you.

Grandma: All my friends show me pictures of their granddaughters with pretty dresses and nice makeup. Yours are always hockey pictures.

Girl: Those other girls are sissies, aren't they Grandma?

★ ★ ★

You might be a Hockey Mom if . . . there's a hockey arena in the background of all your family pictures.

Stranger #1: Are those people crazy?
It's freezing out here.

Stranger #2: They must be in town for
the big hockey tournament.

Free Time

Mom: I feel totally lost. I don't know what to do. Life seems to have no meaning anymore!

Dad: It sounds like you're having a midlife crisis.

Mom: No, I just have a free weekend.

✦ ✦ ✦

Mom: I always wanted to garden.

Dad: Then why don't you?

Mom: The kids aren't gonna drive themselves to those hockey camps!

✦ ✦ ✦

You might be a Hockey Mom if . . . you've had to deal with three children, three tournaments, and three different towns—all on the same day.

It must be hockey season.

Mom's Goalie

Kevin has always been a small kid, so taking to the net was never an easy task for him. Being small has always been his biggest challenge. The first year he played goalie, we thought it would be his last. His team had a 4–19 record going into the postseason.

Ranked last, the team somehow found a way to come together. The coach commended Kevin on being a great team leader and motivator. He took his team from last place to the organization's very first championship.

After winning this championship, Kevin decided to enter the world of rep hockey, signing with a newly formed team. Yet after a disastrous 0–24 season, Kevin was ready to hang up his pads; the coaches felt that he was too small to play.

As Kevin was getting ready to walk away from hockey, he met the coach of his best friend's team. They needed a goalie, and he needed a team. So while the first part of the season got off to a shaky start, his training and drive paid off. His team reached the finals, where they faced off against their biggest rivals. That team had the league's best goal scorer, and we had the league's top goalie.

With our team hanging on to a 1–0 lead to win it all, the other team took a slashing call with .05 seconds left on the clock. A penalty shot was called. The entire rink was holding their breath as the championship came down to the goal scorer and the goalie. Kevin came out of his net aggressively and showed everyone why he was the best in the league. He threw a wicked poke check to kill the penalty shot.

So during his time in minor hockey, he managed to lead two teams that were considered the worst in the league to first-place finishes.

I could not be any more proud of him. He has overcome the odds and continuously gives back to the community. So the saying is true: My favorite goalie calls me Mom.

—Angela,
Hockey Mom

IT'S BROKEN

I'll never forget the time I broke my nose at Madison Square Garden in New York. My trainer had to put two of the long, skinny, white tubes up my nostrils in order to stop the bleeding. Later, they put me up on the jumbo video board with those two cotton things hanging out of my nose.

Apparently, they put me on TV, too, because my mom called me right after the game to make sure I was alright. I was getting asked for a week after if I was okay, so my mom wasn't the only one who saw me on TV looking all beat up!

My mom was always willing to drop everything and drive anywhere at a moment's notice. She was—and still is—awesome!

—Derek Plante,
Hockey Pro
1993–2008

Doctor: Ma'am, I'm sorry to inform you that your son's leg is broken.

Mom: Well, can he skate on it?

HOLIDAYS

Mom: I learned the strangest thing today.

Dad: Oh, really? What's that?

Mom: Thanksgiving is actually a holiday. It's not just a tournament.

✦ ✦ ✦

Mom: Are you excited for Christmas?

Child: Is Christmas home or away this year?

✦ ✦ ✦

Principal: Mrs. Smith, what can I do for you?

Mom: I'm wondering if we can reschedule graduation this year.

Principal: What on earth for?

Mom: Hockey tryouts. My child got a second call back.

Stocking stuffers

Respect

When I think of my mom as a Hockey Mom, I think of her waking me up on those freezing cold, early Saturday mornings to take me to my 7 a.m. game. She'd make my breakfast and try as hard as she could to tie my skates as tight as my dad could. When we had a weekend tournament, she knew that we needed to eat right, so she'd spend all day making meals for me and my brother.

My mom always taught me to show respect for others—especially adults. That translated into me having a good respect for the other players on the ice. My mom is a great woman. She was always there when I needed her. She was and still is someone I can talk to about anything. I love her so much, my mom, Karen Fata!

—Rico Fata,
Hockey Pro
1998–2014

Mom: Say, "Hockey." You can do it. Yes, you can. "Hockey."

HUNGRY

The kids were dressed and ready, so on the ice we went. It was game time.

Things were going well, and my shift was over. But for some reason, instead of heading to the bench, I skated over to the glass where my mom was sitting.

I banged on the glass, saying, "Mom, can you get me a hot dog? I'm starving!"

Everyone laughed.

My mother replied, "No! Get back to the bench. You can have one after the game!"

—Alex Reinert,
Hockey Son

Girl: A sweatshirt? Thanks, Grandma.

Mom: Unless there's a new hockey team called the Teddy Bears, we're gonna have to return that gift.

A SPECIAL VISIT

It was a simple request: Could our Bantam boys swing by a nursing home to visit an avid hockey fan who could no longer travel to a rink? She missed the frenetic pace, the end-to-end action, the crunching body checks, and the passionate cheering from the stands. Without hesitation, our boys were in. When the jersey-clad teens proudly walked into her sterile, quiet room, it wasn't quiet for long. The New York Rangers, Gordie Howe, and Stanley Cup predictions were all part of the nonstop banter. The woman learned all the boys' names, their positions, and their favorite teams. Perhaps our boys didn't know just how much that visit meant to her, but we parents knew. That simple act of kindness was also an important character-building experience—reaffirmed by the note from the senior fan thanking the boys for stirring up "loads of memories."

—Christie Casciano, TV News Anchor,
WSYR-TV Channel 9 New York

Mom's Influence

My mom, Marlene Brodt, taught me how to skate when I was 18 months old. She spent hours at open skating, holding me up on my skates. When I started playing hockey with the boys (there was no girls' hockey then), she spent much of her time driving me and my siblings to practices and to games.

Although my mom is very athletic, there were limited opportunities for women in sports for most of her youth. She began playing recreational hockey when she was in her twenties and still plays today in her sixties. She taught me to never take my opportunities for granted, and I hope that I'm able to continue playing and enjoying the game for years to come. She is the definition of a dedicated Hockey Mom.

—Winny Brodt Brown,
Women's Hockey Pro
2004–Present

BUSY CHATTING

Although my mom loved to watch me play, she never did much watching during the games. She loves to interact and be social. Oftentimes, I'd be talking about a game with my dad, and my mom would mention, "I missed that goal." That's because she was busy chatting away with another mom—or whoever was sitting next to her!

I would not have been successful in hockey without my mom's support and guidance. She played a supportive and emotional role, always making sure that hockey was fun for me and that I enjoyed it. There was no better feeling than to know that my mom was there to guide me, on and off the ice. I'm grateful for all the time, energy, and money that she put in so that I could play hockey.

—Natalie Darwitz,
Women's Hockey Olympian
2002, 2006, 2010

MIKE ERUZIONE

The following is from Jody M. Anderson's interview with hockey legend Mike Eruzione:

When you think of your mom as a Hockey Mom, what comes to mind?

She's somebody who didn't really get involved.

Oh, not like some of the Hockey Moms today?

Very, very opposite of the Hockey Moms today. My mother would take me to practice, drop me off, go home, and come back and get me.

I remember one tournament during my Boston University days. We were playing in the Final Four—now called the Frozen Four—against St. Louis. My mother flew out, but she never watched the game. She sat in the bathroom; she was so nervous! In between periods, she would go out and see how we were doing.

And making sure you weren't hurt?

You know, it's funny: One time, in prep school, I got hit in the face with a stick. It came up and cut me in my forehead, and my mother was right at the end of the rink. I was bleeding and blood was coming down my face. So I skated to the bench and started to wipe the blood off. My mother came out of the stands and behind the bench to see if I was okay. I looked at her and said, "Don't ever do that." She looked at me and then went up in the stands. After the game, my father said, "If I ever hear you talk to your mother like that during a game, you'll be in big trouble." And I ended up getting 10 stitches in my forehead.

Were there any traditions before a game? Like, was your family into the pastas and all of that kind of stuff?

When I was real young, my mother used to give me oranges. She was kind of the "Orange Lady" for the team. She had this little bucket, and she used to cut me oranges. I would take them in the car, and in between periods or after the game, we would have oranges to eat.

How did your mom help to shape you as a player?

There was a ton of support. I played hockey, football, and baseball. My mom was always there for me and supported me. She was always at my games, and she was like that with my brothers, although my sisters weren't into sports. But you know, if I needed something, she seemed to find a way to get it.

We didn't grow up with a lot of money, so it was always hard for me. I remember we would have to pay 50 cents to skate at the practice in the morning. Sometimes I didn't have the 50 cents, so I would owe the 50 cents. But the next week, my mom would always find a way to get me a dollar, so I could pay last week and the next week.

I remember after the Olympics, a reporter was at my house doing a story on me. The guy looked at my mother and said, "You must be very proud of your son."

My mother's answer was, "I'm proud of all my children." And that's how it was.

When I was at Boston University, we had a lot of Canadians on the team and very few Americans. I would have the team come over for dinner. We would take my mother's bed apart and move chairs and tables in there, and my mother would make dinner for the whole team.

When I was playing once in Toledo, Ohio, my mother made dinner in Boston for eight of us, froze it, put it on the plane, brought it to Toledo, and served dinner for the team.

Then in Lake Placid, the parents all stayed in a house. (We called it the hostage house.) My mom made dinner for all the parents. Mr. Christian drove all over Lake Placid to find cheese so my mother could make lasagna. She was very involved with all the parents.

Since your mother couldn't watch your college tournaments, was she there watching the Olympic games?

She went to one game. She flew up, and all night long she got caught in a snowstorm in Washington, DC. It was a nightmare for her, but she got into Lake Placid. She watched the Russian game and then flew out the next day.

Did you even get to see her?

Yes, I did get to see her because after we beat the Russians, they interviewed me in the street. My mother was standing next to me, and my father was standing next to me. It was me, my mom and dad, Jim Craig, and Jim Craig's father. They interviewed us, and it was kind of comical because my mother just stood there and didn't say a word.

Did she think you could win? Was she pretty confident in the team?

We never talked about it. It was always just, "Congratulations," you know, "Good luck," and that was about it.

Mike Eruzione was the captain of the 1980 Winter Olympics United States national hockey team. He and his team famously defeated the Soviet Union in the "Miracle on Ice" game, on their way to a gold medal.

ABOUT JODY

Jody M. Anderson grew up on a 100-acre Quarter Horse farm, where she boarded, trained, showed, and bred horses. Expensive, time-consuming, and with lots of driving, she now knows that this prepared her for life as a Hockey Mom!

Jody has four children, six grandchildren, and one husband. They are the loves of her life. One child played lacrosse in college, another was a diver in college, one played hockey at JR level, and one at HS level. Her son Jeremy is now an assistant high school hockey coach.

Jody's family still enjoys going to professional hockey games and cheering on the local team. Best of all, Jody now has the privilege of watching her six grandchildren play hockey. Life is fabulous!